JAZZ MASTERS

Charlie Christian

by Stan Ayeroff

Consolidated Music Publishers

New York • London • Tokyo • Sydney • Cologne

Cover design by Barbara Hoffman
Back cover photo by Loretta Ayeroff
Edited by Jason Shulman and Peter Pickow

e d c b a

©Consolidated Music Publishers, 1979
A Division of Music Sales Corporation, New York
All Rights Reserved

International Standard Book Number: 0-8256-4084-9

Distributed throughout the world by Music Sales Corporation:

33 West 60th Street, New York 10023
78 Newman Street, London W1P 3LA
4-26-22 Jingumae, Shibuya-ku, Tokyo 150
27 Clarendon Street, Artarmon, Sydney NSW 2064
Kölner Strasse 199, 5000 Cologne 90

Contents

Charlie Christian   4

Notes on the Solos   6

A Note on the Fingering   8

A Note on Swing   8

Explanation of Symbols   8

A Guide to the Charlie Christian Guitar Style   9

    Passing Tones   9

    Grace Notes   9

    Appogiaturas   10

    The Chromatic Scale   10

    Common Positions for Playing off of Chords   11

Playing through Changes   14

As Long as I Live   15

Dinah   16

Good Morning Blues   18

Guy's Got to Go   20

Honeysuckle Rose (I)   23

Honeysuckle Rose (II)   25

Honeysuckle Rose (III)   27

I Can't Give You Anything but Love   29

Ida, Sweet as Apple Cider   30

I Surrender Dear   32

I've Found a New Baby (I)   33

I've Found a New Baby (II)   35

Lips Flips   37

Pagin' the Devil   41

The Sheik of Araby (I)   43

The Sheik of Araby (II)   45

Stardust (I)   47

Stardust (II)   49

Swing to Bop   51

Up on Teddy's Hill   64

Discography   70

Charlie Christian

Because of the proliferation of electric guitars in today's music it is difficult to imagine the excitement generated by the pioneers of the instrument. Though not the first to experiment with the electric guitar, Charlie Christian best understood its inherent possibilities and was the first person to inspire mass acceptance of the instrument. Charlie used the sustaining quality and increased volume of amplification to once and for all lift the guitar from its strict confinement in the rhythm section to the status of a lead horn or soloist.

Jimmy Lunceford's recording of "Hittin' the Bottle" in September 1935 was probably the first recording utilizing any guitar amplification. The tune featured Eddie Durham (Lunceford's trombonist and arranger) on a guitar with a tin resonator. In Leonard Feather's *Book Of Jazz,* Durham recalls:

Lunceford was crazy about the resonator. He used to bring the microphone right up to the F-hole of the guitar, so that between that and the resonator it was almost like having an electric instrument. A year or two later, after the people that made the resonator had gone out of business, I found somebody else who was manufacturing an electrically amplified instrument. I joined Count Basie's band in the summer of 1937 and stayed with him a little over a year. Toward the end of that time I made two sessions with the Kansas City Five and Six, just a few guys out of the Basie band, with Freddie Greene playing rhythm guitar and myself on electric. . . .Touring with the band I ran into Charlie Christian in Oklahoma City. He was playing piano when I first saw him, but I never in my life heard a guy learn to play guitar faster than he did. It was around the latter part of 1937, and I'll never forget that old beat up five-dollar wooden guitar that he took to the jam session where I heard him play. . . . I don't think Christian had ever seen a guitar with an amplifier until he met me. It was a year before they got one on the market generally, and then he got one for himself.

Durham is represented in this book by the transcriptions "Good Morning Blues" and "Pagin' the Devil," both recorded by the Kansas City Six.

It was early in the summer of 1939 that record producer and critic John Hammond stopped off in Oklahoma City to hear the 20-year-old Charlie Christian. He was on his way to California to supervise the first recording sessions Benny Goodman was making under a new Columbia contract. Hammond recollects his impressions in the August 25, 1966 issue of *Downbeat*:

He was carrying on his shoulders a pretty sad combo, including his brother and some other Texans, but the contrast between the never-ending inspiration of Charlie and the mere competence of the others was the most startling I had ever heard. Before an hour had passed, I was determined to place Charlie with Benny Goodman, primarily as a spark for the depleted Goodman quartet.*

It was as a member of the Goodman organization that Charlie gained wide popularity through recordings and radio broadcasts.

The history of jazz guitar begins with the pioneering work of Lonnie Johnson and Eddie Lang. They were the first to develop a single-string technique and establish the guitar as a lead instrument. The great gypsy guitarist, Django Reinhardt, was the next great influence on the instrument. Django's style was developed on acoustic guitar but he was not successful at making the transition to electric instruments, which he experimented with after World War II. The subtleties and nuances which he expressed on the acoustic instrument were lost on the electric. Charlie Christian was the first to develop a technique that was natural to the electric guitar instead of having to adapt an acoustic style. He was the sort of musician that inspires widespread imitation. You can hear his legacy in the playing of almost every guitarist who came after 1939. Why certain jazz styles are inimitable and some are not is an interesting question. Charlie Parker and Charlie Christian have many imitators who in turn spawn their own facsimiles. Others, like Thelonious Monk and Django Reinhardt, appear inimitable, though not because they were more individualistic. In Charlie Christian's case, he laid the blueprint for his instrument's future development by developing a highly idiomatic style.

It is not solely as the progenitor of the electric guitar that Charlie Christian earned his fame in jazz history. Not content to play within the confines of the highly structured Goodman Orchestra and Sextet, Charlie was a frequent participant in the after-hours jam sessions that later led to the development of bebop. At Minton's Playhouse in Harlem, men like Dizzy Gillespie, Charlie Parker, Thelonious Monk, and Kenny Clarke were leading the experiments that would later form a new music. Charlie was such a regular after-hours jammer that he left a spare amp at the club so he could just grab his axe and plug in after his regular gig. Fortunately, some of these sessions were recorded on home equipment, and the transcriptions of "Guy's Got to Go," "Lips Flips," "Swing to Bop," and "Up on Teddy's Hill" show Charlie enjoying the freedom to play chorus after chorus with a never-ending drive and flow of ideas.

It was a tragedy that the beacon that was Charlie Christian burned itself out so quickly. Dead of tuberculosis at the age of twenty-three, he was only on the scene for three years, yet he left his imprint forever in the development of the music he loved—jazz.

---

* Teddy Wilson and Gene Krupa had left to form their own bands.

Notes on the Solos

As Long as I Live

A Benny Goodman Sextet number on which Charlie takes a solo on the middle eight bars of Cootie Williams's trumpet solo.

Dinah

A radio broadcast, by the sextet, of Lionel Hampton's swinging arrangement with a full chorus by Charlie.

Good Morning Blues

From the famous Carnegie Hall concerts of 1938/39 presented by John Hammond. The liner notes list Charlie as the electric guitar soloist along with Count Basie band members Lester Young, Buck Clayton, Freddie Greene, Walter Page, and Jo Jones under the name of the Kansas City Six. In corresponding with Milt Gabler, who actually recorded the concerts, I was informed that Basie trombonist and arranger Eddie Durham was in fact the electric-guitar soloist with the Kansas City Six. The recording was made in 1938 which precedes the recording debut of Charlie Christian by one year.

Guy 's Got to Go

From a jam session taped by jazz enthusiast Jerry Newman at Clark Monroe's Uptown House in 1941. Monroe's, along with Minton's Playhouse, provided the space in which musicians could develop and test out new ideas about music. It was at jam sessions like this that the music later known as *bebop* emerged.

This tune was named after trumpeter Joe Guy, a member of the house band at Minton's and a frequent participant in the sessions. The recordings were made on primitive equipment and the quality is poor. Originally issued on the Esoteric label, the engineers edited heavily, making many splices and adjustments to remove unwanted noise. In this particular song the editing has created some strange moments. In measure 16 there are two beats missing, creating a $\frac{2}{4}$ measure. Measure 33 has one extra quarter note (B$\flat$) creating a $\frac{5}{4}$ measure.

Honeysuckle Rose (I)

Charlie takes a full chorus in the Goodman Orchestra's performance of Fletcher Henderson's big-band arrangement.

Honesuckle Rose (II)

Charlie takes a chorus on a radio broadcast by the Benny Goodman Septet.

Honeysuckle Rose (III)

This version, by the sextet, is from the 1939 Carnegie Hall concert presented by John Hammond.

I Can't Give You Anything but Love

The septet performance of this old standard features Charlie on a half chorus.

Ida, Sweet as Apple Cider

A radio broadcast of the septet with a full chorus by Charlie.

I Surrender Dear

A sextet recording with a half chorus by Charlie.

I've Found a New Baby (I)

The septet with a chorus by Charlie.

I've Found a New Baby (II)

An alternate take.

Lips Flips

Another jam session recording named after trumpter and vocalist Hot Lips Page.

Pagin' the Devil

Another recording of the Kansas City Six probably featuring Eddie Durham rather than Charlie on electric guitar.

The Sheik of Araby (I)

Sextet recording with a chorus by Charlie.

The Sheik of Araby (II)

An alternate recording of a radio broadcast.

Stardust (I)

This transcription covers the first chorus of a privately-cut recording (made by a disc jockey during a live performance in a Minneapolis club in March 1940). The second chorus (which I have transcribed as "Stardust (II)") is a planned solo performed almost note for note on CBS 62 581 recorded on October 2, 1939, and Musidisc 30 JA 5181 recorded on October 9, 1939.

Stardust (II)

CBS 62 581 recording of Charlie's version of this standard which greatly impressed Benny Goodman.

Swing to Bop

Another jam session on which Charlie really gets a chance to stretch out. The transcription starts on the first bridge.

Up on Teddy's Hill

Named for bandleader Teddy Hill, who became the manager of Minton's, this jam session tune is based on the chord progression of "Honeysuckle Rose."

A Note on the Fingering

I have attempted to use those fingerings that were the most facile while producing the desired sound. There are many choices of which these are the ones that worked best for me. The reader may find that another fingering suits his particular technique better than the one I have chosen. If so, feel free to experiment.

A Note on Swing

In all of the transcriptions, eighth notes are to be played in a swing manner. This means that two eighth notes ♪♪ are to be played as the first and third notes of a triplet.

If the words *straight rhythm* are written above a series of notes, play them without a swing feel (as written).

Explanation of Symbols

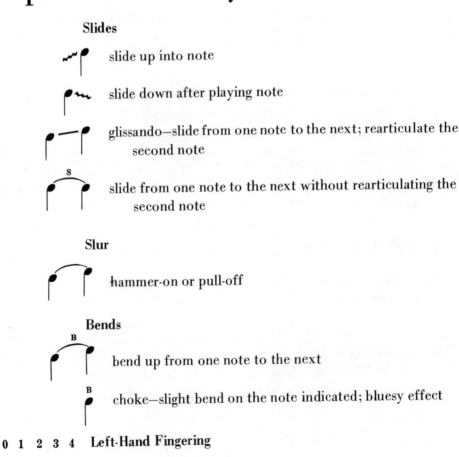

Slides

slide up into note

slide down after playing note

glissando—slide from one note to the next; rearticulate the second note

slide from one note to the next without rearticulating the second note

Slur

hammer-on or pull-off

Bends

bend up from one note to the next

choke—slight bend on the note indicated; bluesy effect

0 1 2 3 4   **Left-Hand Fingering**

① ② ③ ④ ⑤ ⑥   **String Numbers**

A Guide to the Charlie Christian Guitar Style

Although it is not the intention of this book to deal extensively with basic chord construction and counterpoint, this section presents several positions and concepts used most often throughout the solos that follow. This should serve as an aid to understanding and playing the music of Charlie Christian. The reader is strongly encouraged to fill in any gaps with supplementary instruction and reading.

First, a word about certain contrapuntal devices used throughout the solos.

Passing Tones (P.T.)

1. Scalewise—fill in the notes of the chromatic scale between chord tones.

2. Chromatic—fill in the notes of the chromatic scale between chord tones.

Note: Usually a passing tone falls on a weak beat or weak part of the beat, however, it is characteristic of Charlie Christian's style to play *accented passing tones* (falling on a strong beat or strong part of the beat).

Grace Notes (G.N.)

Very often the ♯2nd is played before the major 3rd.

Less often the major 7th is played before the root.

Sometimes the 6th acts as a *grace note* to the ♭ 7th.

Appogiaturas (App.)

The 4th often precedes the grace note figure, ♯ 2nd to 3rd.

Charlie Christian made extensive used of the chromatic scale. The chart that follows will attempt to show how it is possible to use all twelve notes of the chromatic scale.

The Chromatic Scale
Functions of Each Scale Degree as Related to a C Chord

C Root (chord tone)

C♯ D♭ chromatic passing tone between root and 9th

D♭ ♭9 (chord tone)

D 9th (chord tone); also functions as 2nd—scalewise passing tone between root and 3rd

D♯ E♭ chromatic passing tone between 9th and 10th (3rd)

E♭ ♭3rd (blues note); also chord tone in minor chord

E 3rd (chord tone)

F appogiatura 4th usually followed by ♯2nd to 3rd; also scalewise passing tone between 3rd and 5th

F♯ G♭ chromatic passing tone (when preceded by 4th) between 3rd and 5th; e.g., E F F♯ G

G♭ ♭5th (blues note)

G 5th (chord tone)

G♯ A♭ chromatic passing tone between 5th and 6th

G♯ ♯5th (altered chord tone)

A 6th (chord tone); sometimes grace note to ♭7th

B♭ ♭7th (blues note)

B major 7th (chord tone in major 7th chord); sometimes a grace note to root

C♭ chromatic passing tone between root and ♭7th

Common Positions for Playing off of Chords

Major Chord (Tonic)

F major
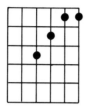

Added Chord Tones
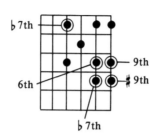

Ornaments
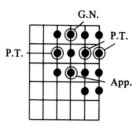

F major
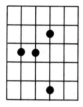

Added Chord Tones
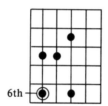

Ornaments
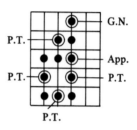

D major
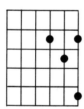

Added Chord Tones
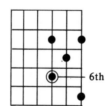

Ornaments
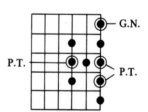

A major
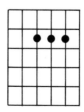

Added Chord Tones
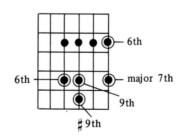

Ornaments
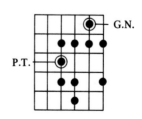

Dominant 7th Chords

F7
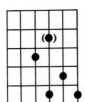

Added Chord Tones
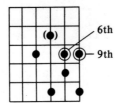

— 6th
— 9th

Ornaments
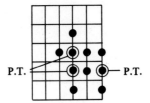

P.T. —   — P.T.

B7
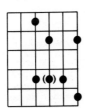

Added Chord Tones
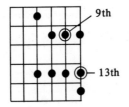

— 9th
— 13th

Ornaments
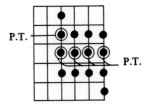

P.T. —   — P.T.

Extra Dominant Positions

G9
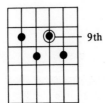

— 9th

F7/6
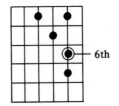

— 6th

Minor Chords

Bm

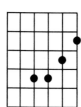

Added Chord Tones

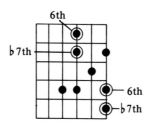

Ornaments

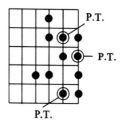

F♯m

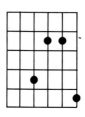

Added Chord Tones

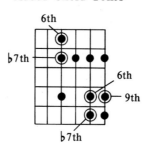

Ornaments

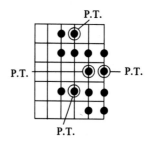

Em

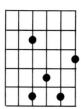

Added Chord Tones

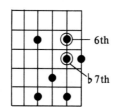

Ornaments

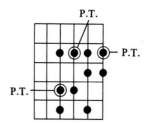

Playing through Changes

Charlie Christian was a master at playing *through* a series of chords, often a cycle of 5ths type of progression. He did this by connecting the various positions illustrated in a smooth and exciting manner. He often anticipated the approaching chord during the previous one (*anticipation—ant.*) creating a feeling of great drive. Throughout the solos you will find extensive use of the interval of the tritone (♯4th) to chromatically connect a series of 7th chords.

Here is an excerpt from "I Can't Give You Anything but Love" illustrating many of the points discussed in this section.

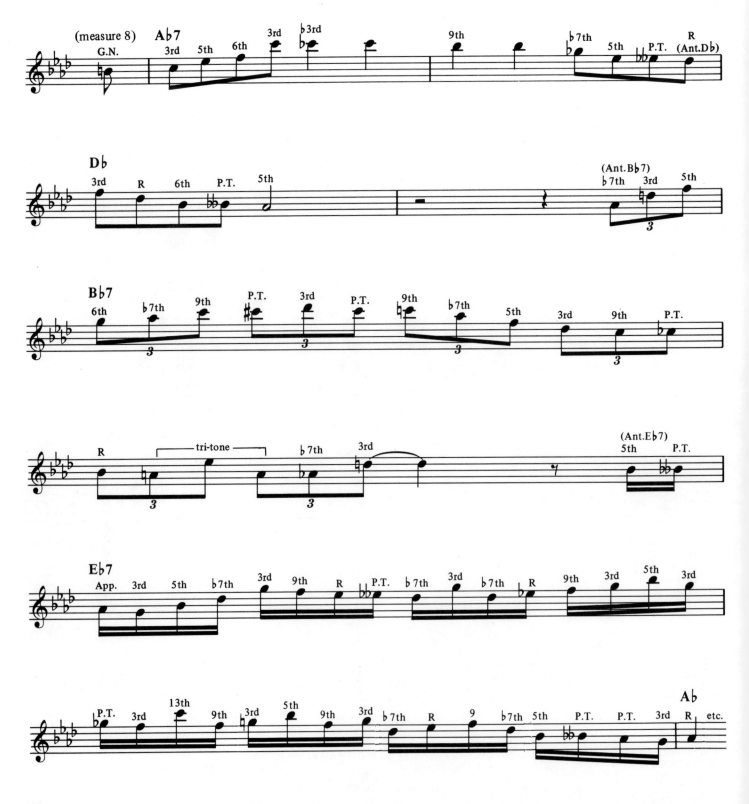

As Long as I Live

Words by Ted Koehler
Music by Harold Arlen

(solo middle eight only)

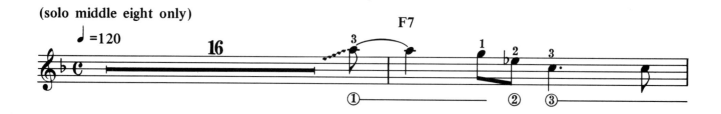

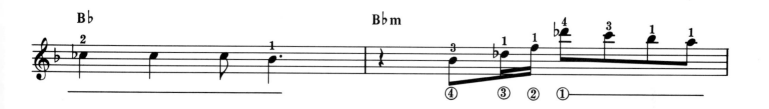

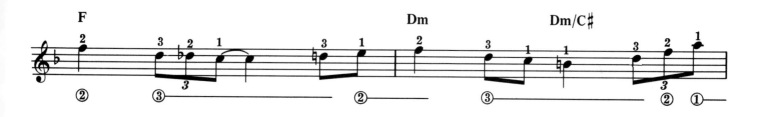

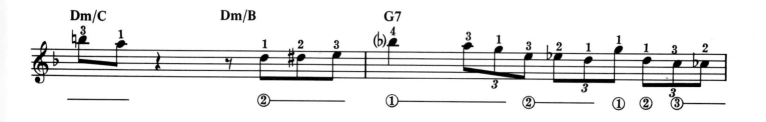

Dinah

by Sam Lewis, Joe Young, and Harry Akst

Good Morning Blues

Lyrics by James Rushing
Music by Count Basie and Ed Durham

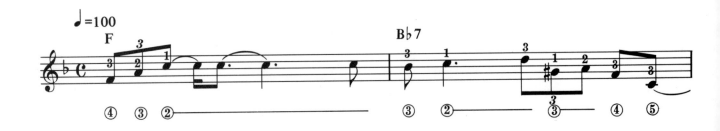

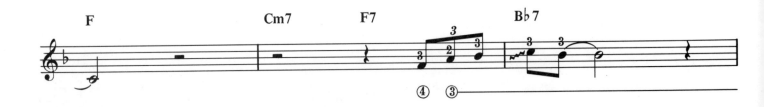

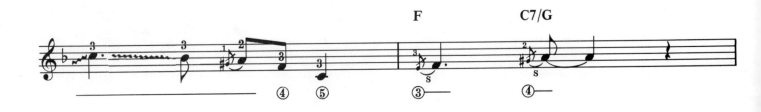

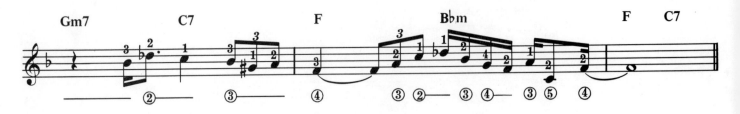

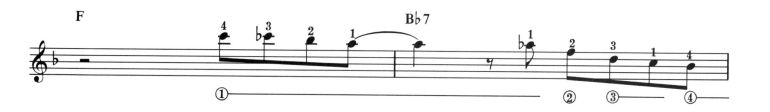

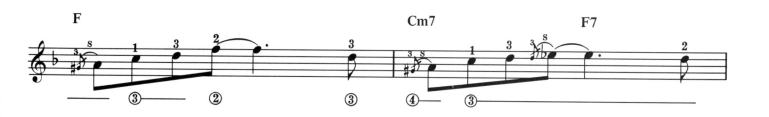

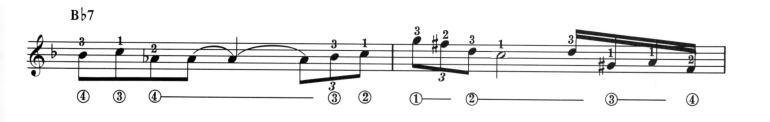

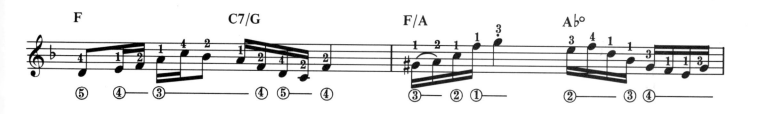

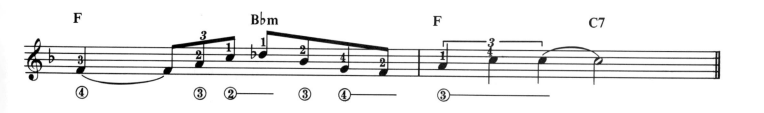

Guy's Got to Go

Honeysuckle Rose (I)

by Fats Waller and Andy Razaf

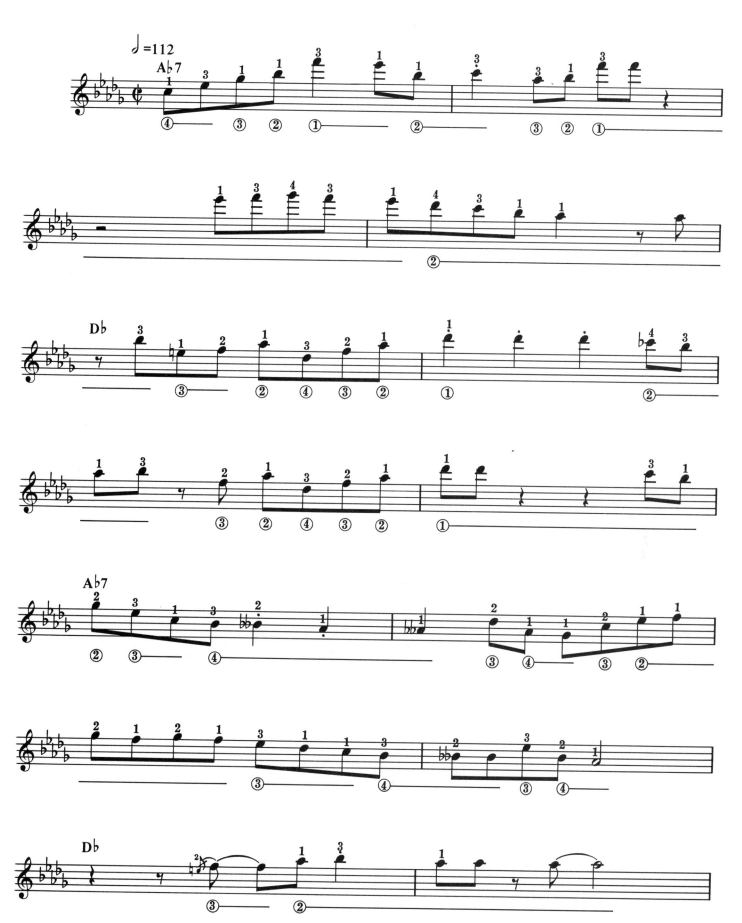

24

Honeysuckle Rose (II)

by Fats Waller and Andy Razaf

Honeysuckle Rose (III)

by Fats Waller and Andy Razaf

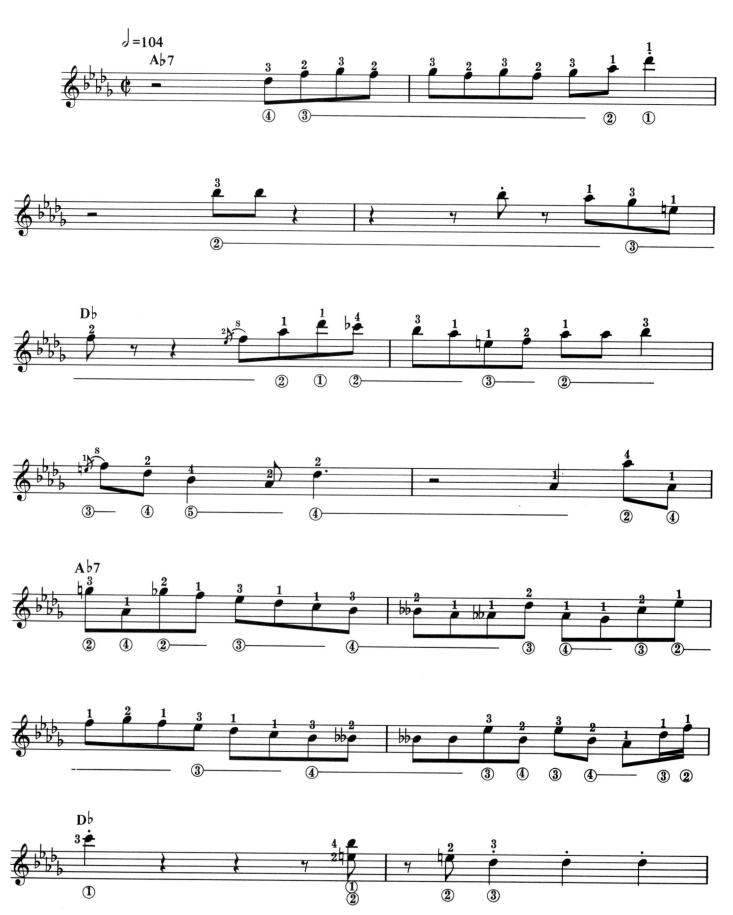

I Can't Give You Anything but Love

by Dorothy Fields
and Jimmy McHugh

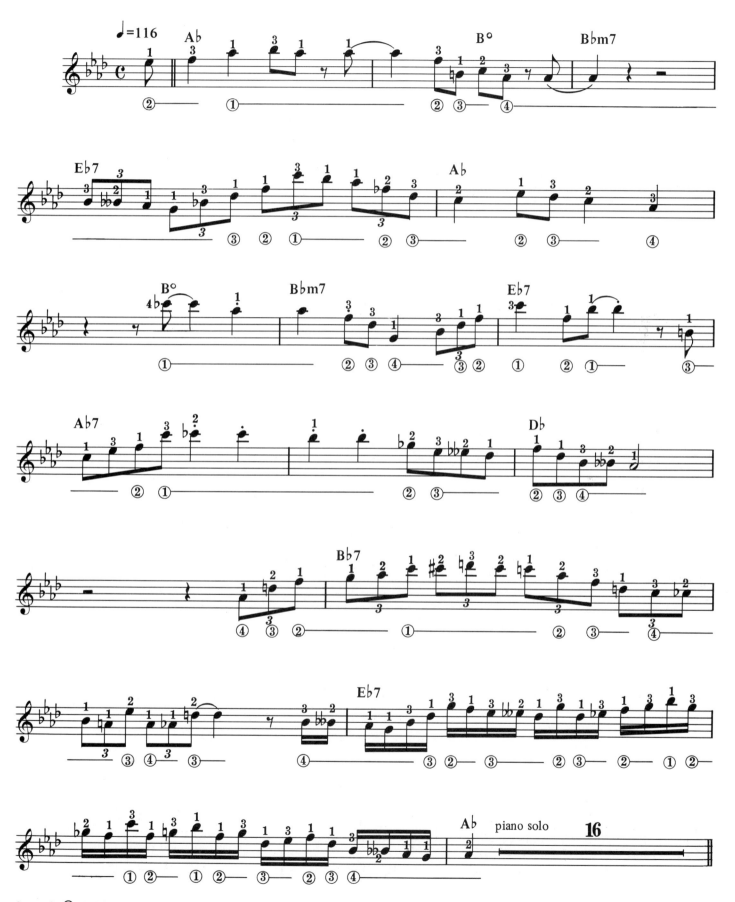

Ida, Sweet as Apple Cider

Lyrics by Eddie Leonard
Music by Eddie Munson

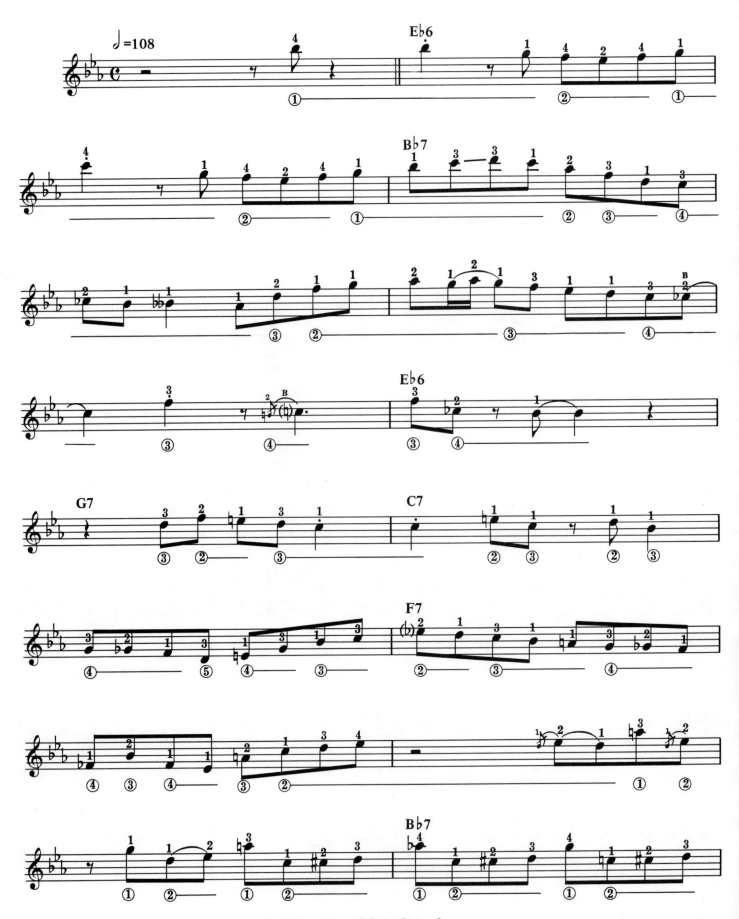

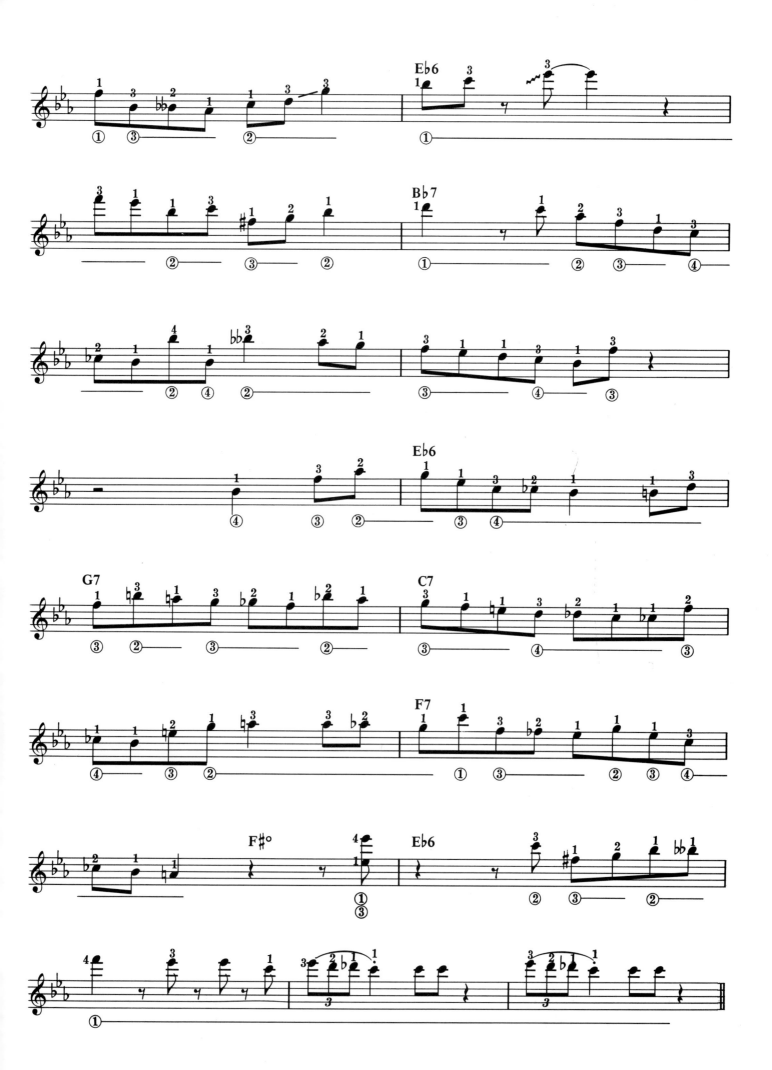

I Surrender Dear

by Gordon Clifford and Harry Barris

I've Found a New Baby (I)

Words and Music by
Jack Palmer and Spencer Williams

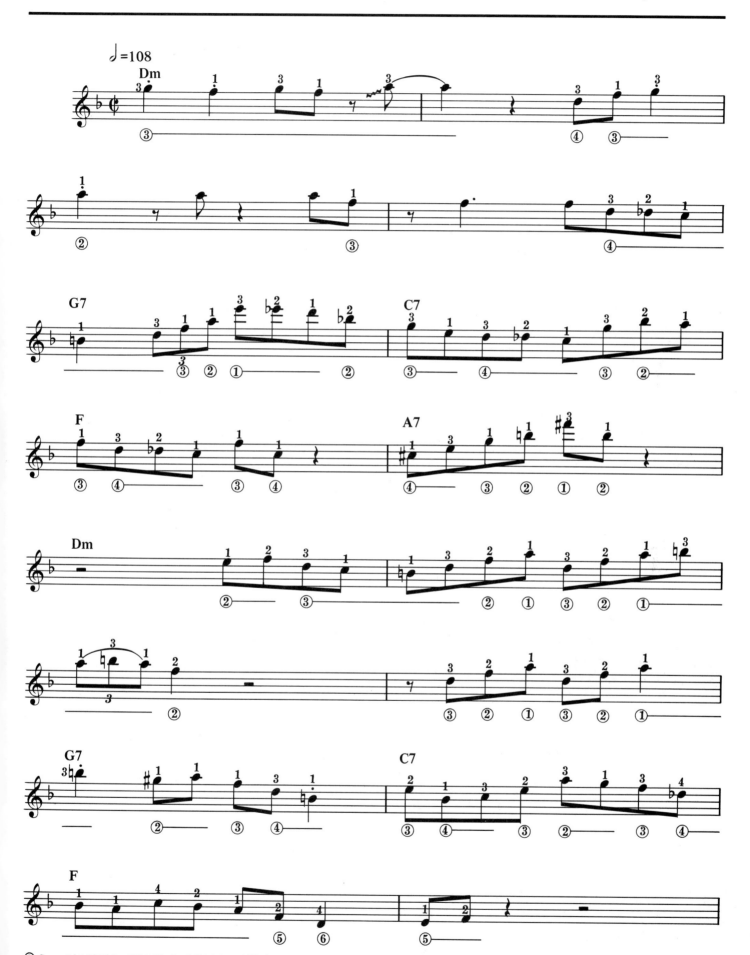

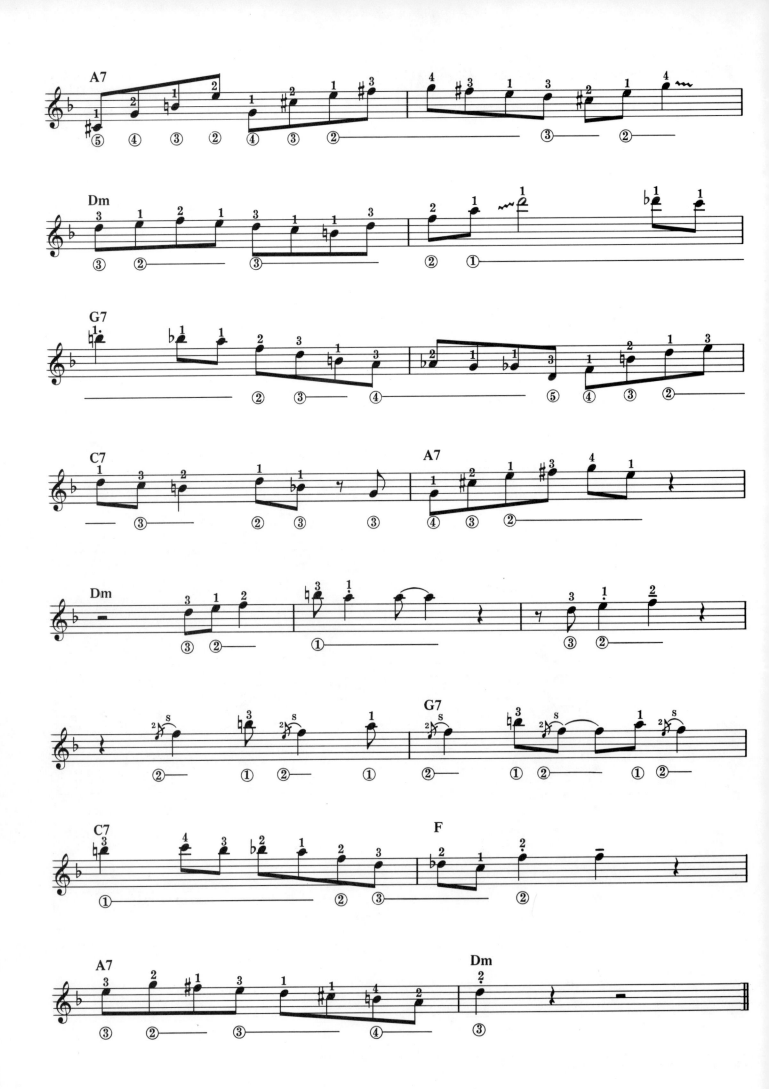

I've Found a New Baby (II)

Words and Music by
Jack Palmer and Spencer Williams

Lips Flips

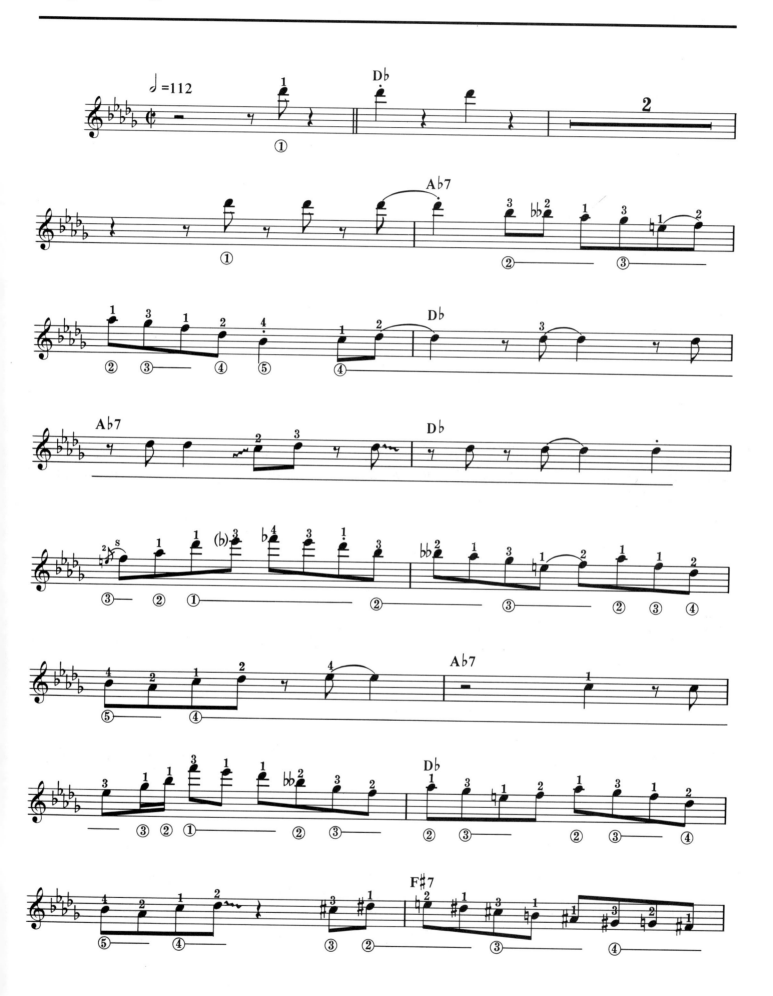

Pagin' the Devil

by Walter Page and Milt Gabler

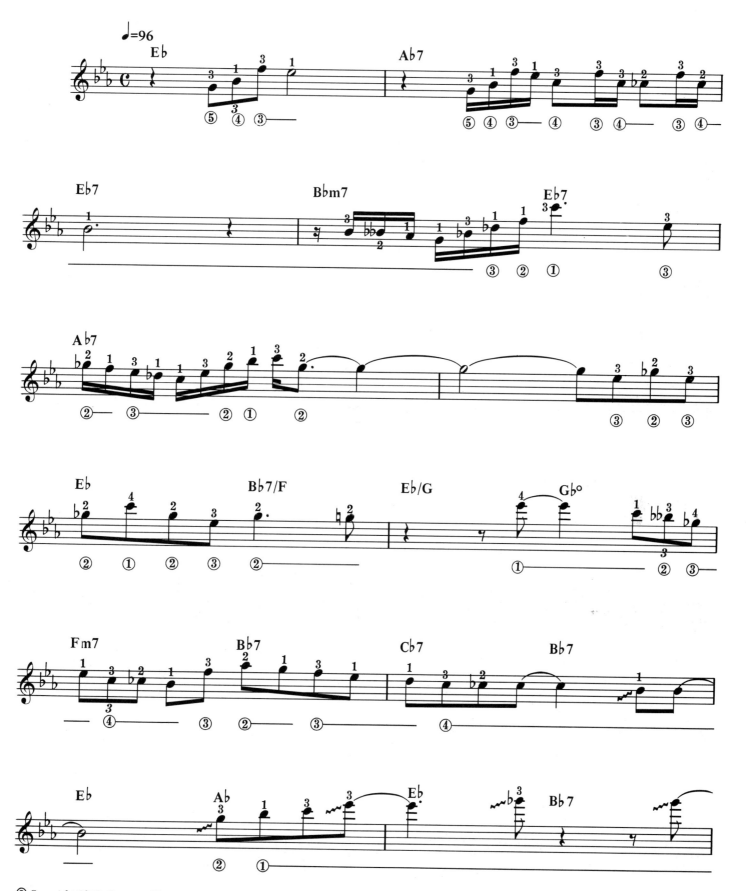

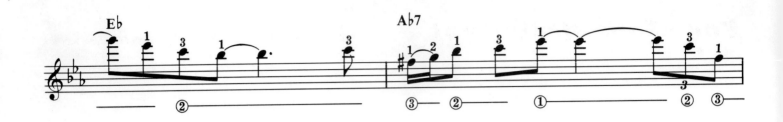

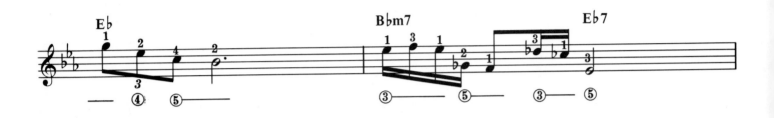

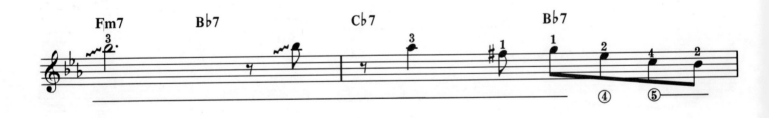

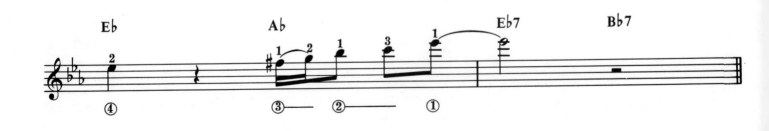

The Sheik of Araby (I)

by Harry B. Smith, Francis Wheeler, and Ted Snyder

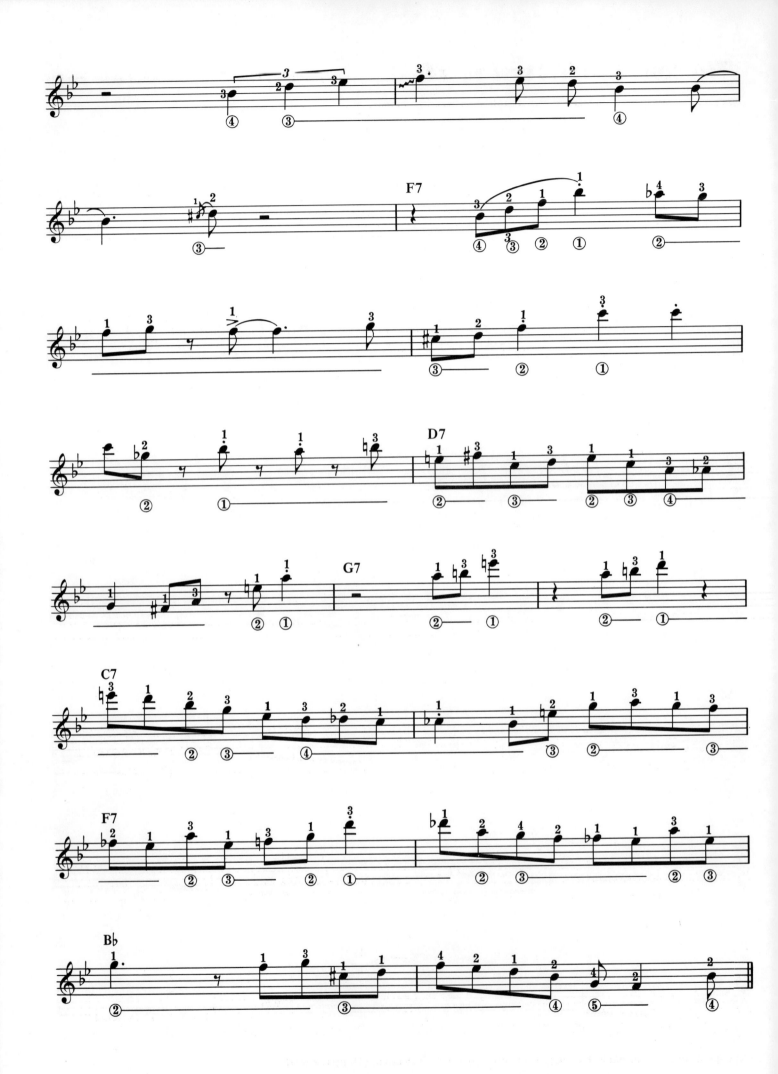

The Sheik of Araby (II)

by Harry B. Smith, Francis Wheeler, and Ted Snyder

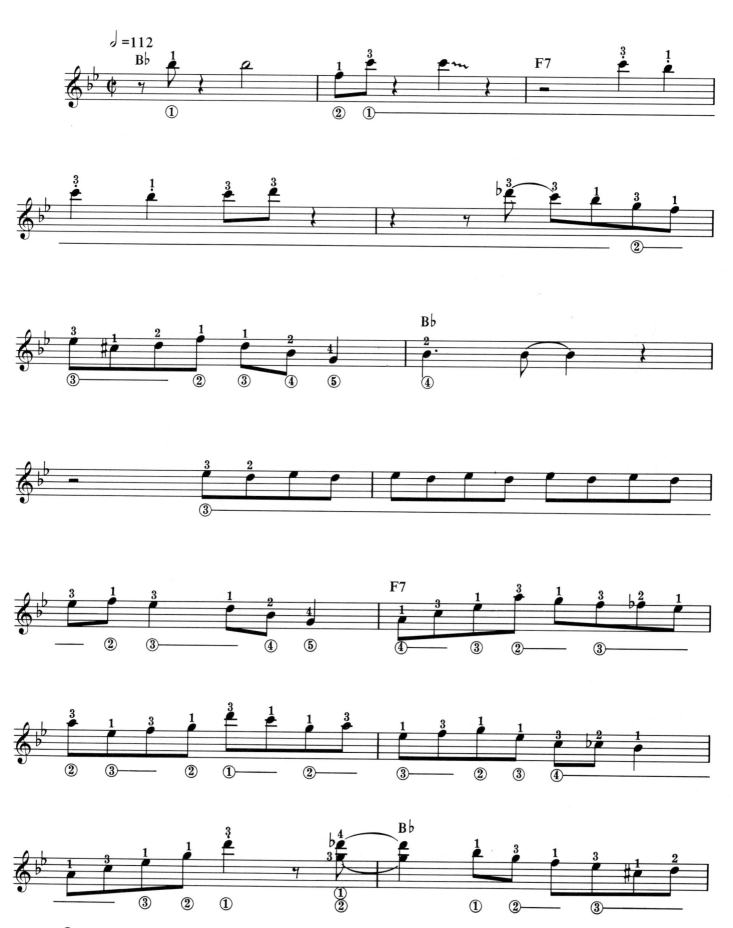

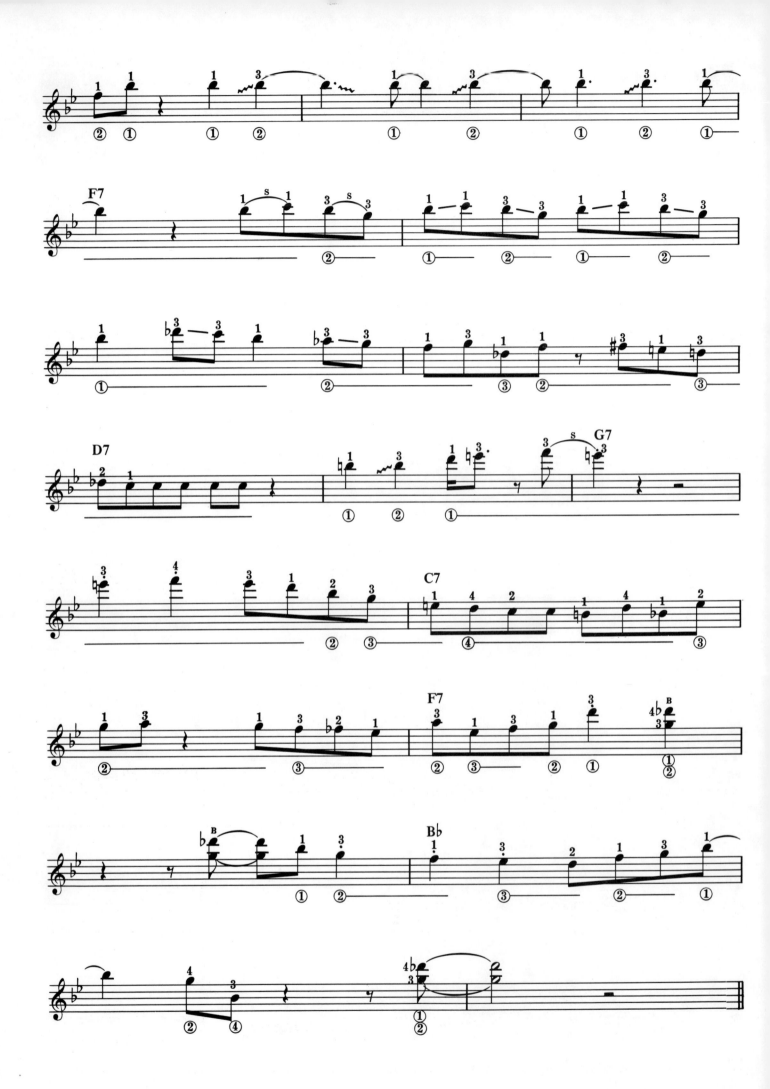

Stardust (I)

by Hoagy Carmichael and Mitchell Parish

Stardust (II)

by Hoagy Carmichael and Mitchell Parish

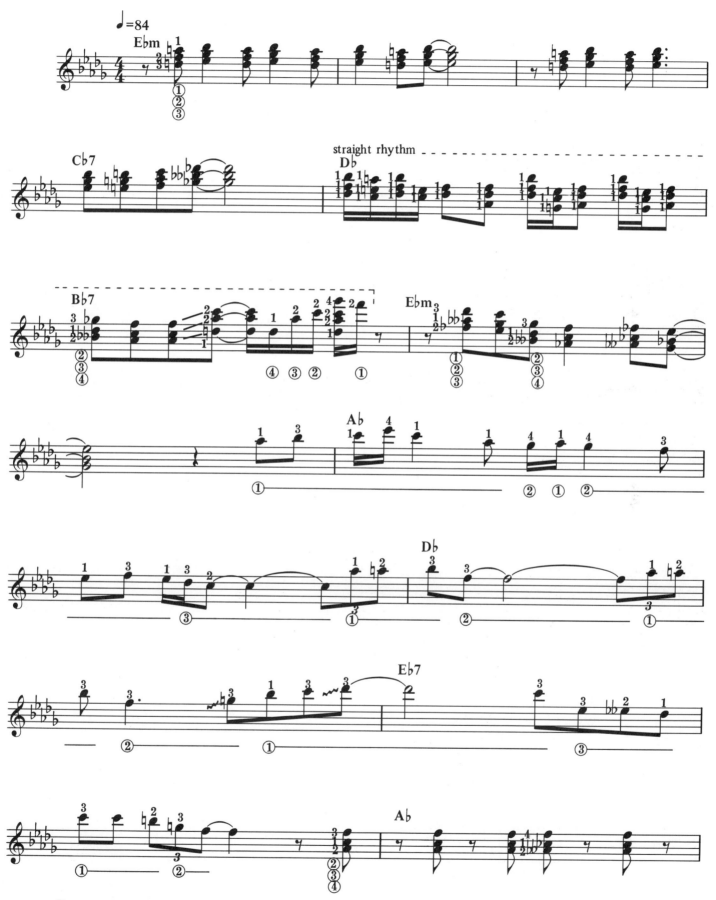

Swing to Bop

58

Up on Teddy's Hill

Discography

The following is a discography of Charlie Christian's recorded output. Some albums are imports and some are out of print. Either write the record company or look in the vintage jazz section of your nearest major record store (or one that specializes in rare and out-of-print jazz albums).

Solo Flight—The Genius of Charlie Christian
Columbia CG 30779, John Hammond Collection.
"As Long as I Live," "Honeysuckle Rose (I)," "I Can't Give You Anything but Love," "I've Found a New Baby (II)," "Stardust (I)."

Charlie Christian With The Benny Goodman Sextet And Orchestra
Columbia CL 652.

Solo Flight—Charlie Christian With The Benny Goodman Sextet, Septet, and Orchestra
CBS (Columbia), *Aimez-Vous le Jazz no. 3* 62-581. (Printed in Holland)
"As Long as I Live," "Honeysuckle Rose (I)," "I Can't Give You Anything but Love," "I've Found a New Baby (I)," "I Surrender Dear," "Stardust (II)," "The Sheik of Araby (I)."

John Hammond's Spirituals To Swing—The Legendary Carnegie Hall Concerts of 1938/9
Vanguard (s) VRS 8523/4
"Good Morning Blues," "Honeysuckle Rose (III)," "Pagin' the Devil."

Charlie Christian—Archive of Folk Music — Jazz Series
Everest FS-219
Write for information to Everest Records, 10920 Wilshire Blvd., Suite 410, L.A., California 90024.
"Guy's Got to Go," "Lips Flips," "Swing to Bop," "Up on Teddy's Hill."

Charlie Christian Live 1939/1941—Jazz Anthology
Musidisc 30 JA 5181. (Printed in France)
"Dinah," "Honeysuckle Rose (II)," "Ida, Sweet as Apple Cider," "The Sheik of Araby (II)."